Thank you...

... for purchasing this copy of Get Ready for Year 5.

We hope that you will find this book helpful in preparing your child to move up to their next year-group. You may choose to use it during the final few months of Year 4, during the summer holidays or in the first few months of Year 5.

On our Teachers and Parents pages we summarise the likely content of each subject in Year 5. On the children's pages we feature activities that will help prepare children for most of their subjects, hopefully giving them confidence to take part in their lessons with enthusiasm, skills and knowledge.

This book is part of our growing range of educational titles. Most of our books are individual workbooks but, due to popular demand, we are now introducing a greater number of photocopiable titles for teachers.

To find details of our other publications, please visit our website:

www.andrewbrodie.co.uk

CONTENTS

During the course of Year 5, pupils will:

- ✓ learn the effects of multiplying whole numbers by 10 or 100;
- ✓ learn the effect of dividing whole numbers by 10 or 100;
- ✓ write positive and negative whole numbers in order of size;
- ✓ begin to use decimals;
- ✓ round numbers with one or two decimal places to the nearest whole number;
- ✓ learn the relationship between fractions and division;
- ✓ use mental arithmetic for calculating differences such as 7004 – 3991;
- ✓ complete addition and subtraction questions by setting numbers out in columns. They will need to be able to calculate quickly by knowing number facts, such as 7 + 9, thoroughly and by knowing doubles and halves;
- ✓ learn all the multiplication tables up to 10 x 10;
- ✓ multiply three-digit numbers by single-digit numbers;
- ✓ divide three-digit numbers by two-digit numbers;
- ✓ multiply two-digit numbers by two-digit numbers;
- ✓ learn about measuring area in square centimetres, using the formula 'length x breadth' for rectangles; learn how to find the perimeter of shapes;
- ✓ work with parallel and perpendicular lines;
- ✓ solve word problems, including those related to measurements and time. Pupils will need to know how many centimetres are in one metre, how many days are in each month, etc.

TEACHERS & PARENTS

DIFFERENT WAYS OF CALCULATING

Ultimately most schools will teach pupils the 'traditional' methods of calculating for the four operations of addition, subtraction, multiplication and division:

Examples:

$$\begin{array}{r} 326 \\ +\ 149 \\ \hline 475 \\ \hline {\scriptstyle 1} \end{array} \qquad \begin{array}{r} {\scriptstyle 2\ \ 11\ \ 1} \\ \not{3}\not{2}6 \\ -\ 149 \\ \hline 177 \\ \hline \end{array} \qquad \begin{array}{r} 326 \\ \times\ \ \ 4 \\ \hline 1304 \\ \hline {\scriptstyle 1\ \ 2\ } \end{array} \qquad \begin{array}{r} 163 \\ 2\overline{)3^{1}26} \end{array}$$

However, schools will also use other very good methods to help children to understand the processes:

Examples:

Addition

$$\begin{array}{rl} 326 & \\ +\ 149 & \\ \hline 400 & (300 + 100) \\ 60 & (20 + 40) \\ 15 & (6 + 9) \\ \hline 475 & \\ \hline \end{array}$$

Subtraction

$$\begin{array}{rl} 326 & \\ -\ 149 & \\ \hline 51 & (149 + 51 = 200) \\ 100 & (200 + 100 = 300) \\ 26 & (300 + 26 = 326) \\ \hline 177 & \\ \hline \end{array}$$

This method shows how to add on to the lower number to reach the higher number.

Multiplication

59 x 37

x	50	9		
30	1500	270	→	1770
7	350	63	→	413
				2183

Division

375 ÷ 8

$$\begin{array}{rl} 326 & \\ -\ 160 & 20 \times 8 \\ \hline 215 & \\ 160 & 20 \times 8 \\ \hline 55 & \\ 48 & 6 \times 8 \\ \hline 7 & \end{array}$$

Answer: 46 remainder 7

The school will decide which method is best suited to the children's mathematical development. Teachers are usually very happy to discuss the methods they are using.

MULTIPLYING BY 10 OR 100

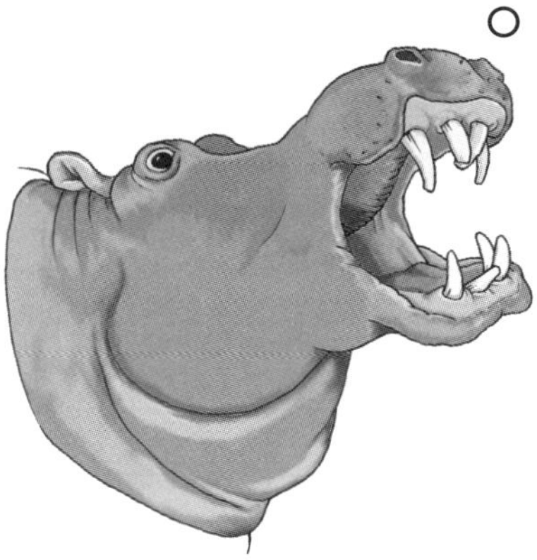

Look what happens when you multiply by ten.

4 x 10 = 40

4 units....multiplied by 10....moves the 4 into the tens column

52 x 10 = 520

5 tens — 2 units — 5 hundreds and 2 tens

Fill in the missing numbers:

(a) 4 x 10 = ☐	(b) 34 x 10 = ☐	(c) 25 x 10 = ☐
(d) 99 x 10 = ☐	(e) 16 x 10 = ☐	(f) 50 x 10 = ☐
(g) 700 x 10 = ☐	(h) 6000 x 10 = ☐	
(i) ☐ x 10 = 70	(j) ☐ x 10 = 580	(k) ☐ x 10 = 190

(l) ☐ x 10 = 1000000 ← Did you know that this number is one million?

Look what happens when you multiply by 100.

6 x 100 = 600

6 units....multiplied by 100....moves the 6 into the hundreds column

(m) 8 x 100 = ☐	(n) 4 x 100 = ☐	(o) 16 x 100 = ☐
(p) 48 x 100 = ☐	(q) 79 x 100 = ☐	(r) 40 x 100 = ☐
(s) ☐ x 10 = 900	(t) ☐ x 10 = 9600	(u) ☐ x 100=10000

PRACTISING MULTIPLICATION TABLES

1 x 7 = 7	One seven is seven
2 x 7 = 14	Two sevens are fourteen
3 x 7 = 21	Three sevens are twenty-one
4 x 7 = 28	Four sevens are twenty-eight
5 x 7 = 35	Five sevens are thirty-five
6 x 7 = 42	Six sevens are forty-two
7 x 7 = 49	Seven sevens are forty-nine
8 x 7 = 56	Eight sevens are fifty-six
9 x 7 = 63	Nine sevens are sixty-three
10 x 7 = 70	Ten sevens are seventy

Say your tables as you write them:

1 x 2 = 2	1 x 3 = 3	1 x 4 = 4
=	=	=
=	=	=
=	=	=
=	=	=
=	=	=
=	=	=
=	=	=
=	=	=
=	=	=

1 x 5 = 5	1 x 6 = 6	1 x 7 = 7
=	=	=
=	=	=
=	=	=
=	=	=
=	=	=
=	=	=
=	=	=
=	=	=
=	=	=

MORE MULTIPLICATION TABLES PRACTICE

1 x 8 = 8	1 x 9 = 9	1 x 10 = 10
=	=	=
=	=	=
=	=	=
=	=	=
=	=	=
=	=	=
=	=	=
=	=	=
=	=	=

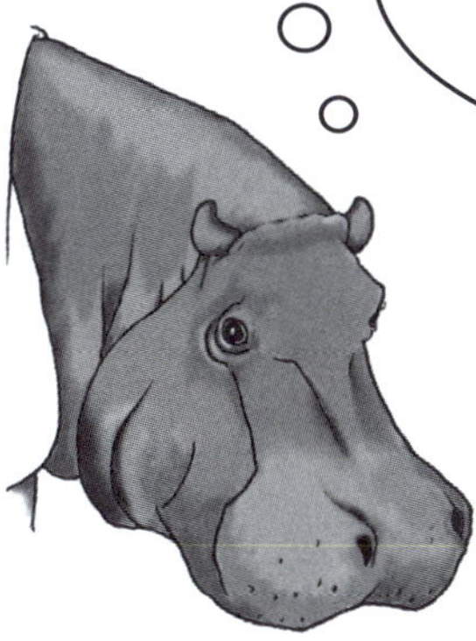

We can use our tables to help us answer division questions.

For example, twelve divided by three is four because three fours are twelve.

a.	32 ÷ 4 =		a.	28 ÷ 4 =		a.	36 ÷ 6 =	
b.	48 ÷ 6 =		b.	30 ÷ 5 =		b.	64 ÷ 8 =	
c.	20 ÷ 5 =		c.	24 ÷ 3 =		c.	4 ÷ 2 =	
d.	81 ÷ 9 =		d.	42 ÷ 6 =		d.	81 ÷ 9 =	
e.	40 ÷ 8 =		e.	18 ÷ 6 =		e.	16 ÷ 4 =	
f.	36 ÷ 9 =		f.	27 ÷ 3 =		f.	49 ÷ 7 =	
g.	21 ÷ 7 =		g.	36 ÷ 4 =		g.	9 ÷ 3 =	
h.	16 ÷ 2 =		h.	45 ÷ 5 =		h.	25 ÷ 5 =	
i.	32 ÷ 8 =		i.	56 ÷ 7 =		i.	100 ÷ 10 =	
j.	54 ÷ 6 =		j.	72 ÷ 8 =		j.	1 ÷ 1 =	
Time taken			Time taken			Time taken		

POSITIVE AND NEGATIVE NUMBERS

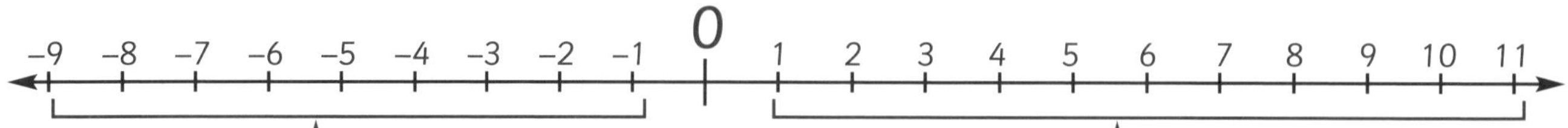

These are all negative numbers.
They are below zero.

These are all positive numbers.
They are above zero.

You can find positive and negative numbers on a thermometer.

When the weather is very cold there might be a temperature of minus three degrees. This is three degrees below zero.

Here are some positive and negative numbers: 7 –4 4 9 –8 –1

Estimate where the numbers should go on this line:

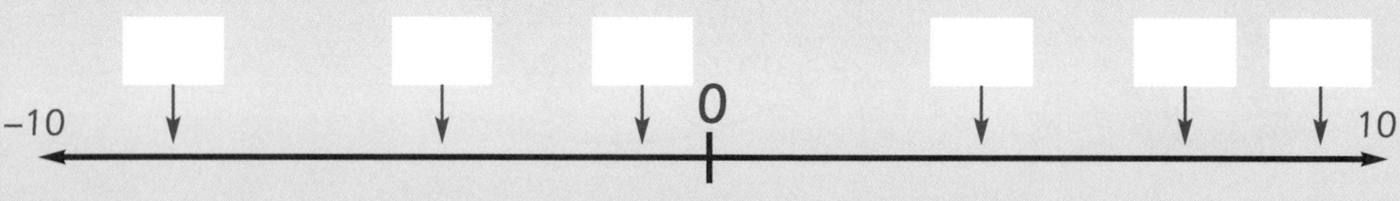

Here is a different number line:

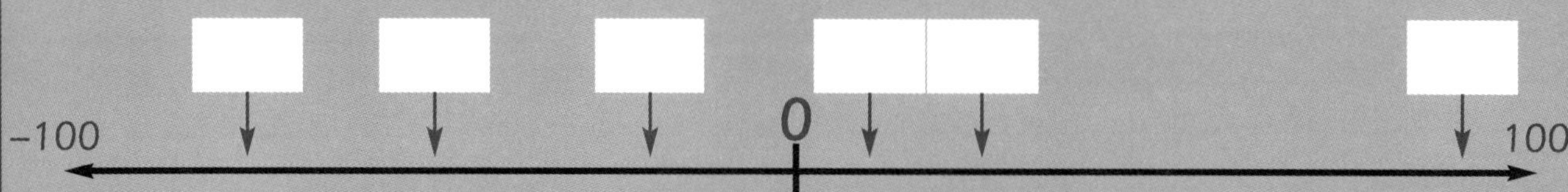

Write these numbers in the correct places.

–50 25 –75 10 90 –20

Look at this number line:

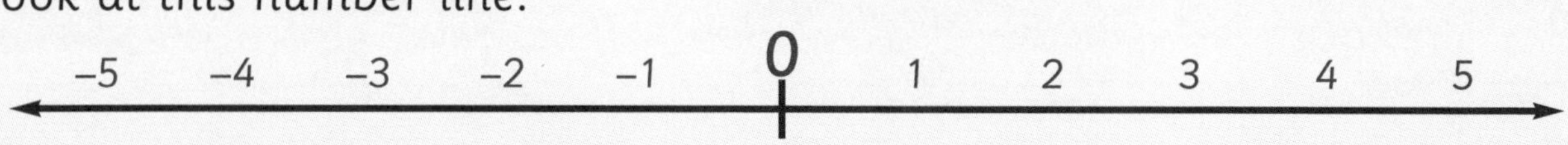

To get from –3 to 3, we need to jump 3 places to zero then 3 more to 3.
We have jumped 6 places altogether.
How many places is it from –2 to 5?

MONTHS AND YEARS

> Thirty days has September,
> April, June and November.
> All the rest have thirty-one,
> Except for February alone,
> Which has twenty-eight days clear
> And twenty-nine in each leap year.

What's a leap year?

A leap year is a year which has an extra day in February. It happens every four years.

Use the rhyme to help you to fill in the number of days for each month:

January		February		March	
April		May		June	
July		August		September	
October		November		December	

Which months have 30 days?

Which months have 31 days?

How many days are there normally in one year?

How many days are there in a leap year?

Do you know the answers to these questions?

You could use a dictionary to help you.

How many years are there in a decade?

How many years are there in a century?

How many years are there in a millennium?

FAST WORK

Answer the questions in the shapes as quickly as you can.

Quick Subtractions

a. 27 – 8 = ☐	b. 32 – 6 = ☐	c. 14 – 3 = ☐
d. 16 – 9 = ☐	e. 17 – 8 = ☐	f. 13 – 6 = ☐
g. 40 – 8 = ☐	h. 40 – 18 = ☐	i. 40 – 28 = ☐
j. 40 – 38 = ☐	k. 100 – 50 = ☐	l. 100 – 51 = ☐

This shape is a ______ Time taken ____ seconds.

Quick Additions

a. 6 + 9 = ☐	b. 7 + 5 = ☐
c. 9 + 7 = ☐	d. 8 + 4 = ☐
e. 7 + 8 = ☐	f. 17 + 8 = ☐
g. 27 + 8 = ☐	h. 67 + 8 = ☐
i. 4 + 9 = ☐	j. 24 + 9 = ☐
k. 84 + 9 = ☐	l. 94 + 9 = ☐

This shape is a ______

Time taken ____ seconds.

Quick Doubles

a. 6 + 6 = ☐

b. 9 + 9 = ☐

c. 5 + 5 = ☐

d. 12 + 12 = ☐	e. 14 + 14 = ☐
f. 20 + 20 = ☐	g. 15 + 15 = ☐
h. 50 + 50 = ☐	i. 25 + 25 = ☐

This shape is a ______

Time taken ____ seconds.

Fast Work

MORE FAST WORK

Quick Halves

Time taken ☐ seconds.

a. $\frac{1}{2}$ of 20 = ☐

b. $\frac{1}{2}$ of 30 = ☐ c. $\frac{1}{2}$ of 40 = ☐

d. $\frac{1}{2}$ of 50 = ☐ e. $\frac{1}{2}$ of 60 = ☐

f. $\frac{1}{2}$ of 70 = ☐ g. $\frac{1}{2}$ of 80 = ☐

h. $\frac{1}{2}$ of 90 = ☐ i. $\frac{1}{2}$ of100= ☐

j. $\frac{1}{2}$ of 26 = ☐

k. $\frac{1}{2}$ of 28 = ☐

l. $\frac{1}{2}$ of 36 = ☐

This shape is a ☐

Quick Mixture

a. 7 + 3 = ☐

b. 8 + 5 = ☐

c. 28 + 4 = ☐

d. 42 – 7 = ☐ e. 7 x 9 = ☐

f. 8 x 6 = ☐ g. 56 ÷ 7 = ☐

h. 100 ÷ 20 = ☐

i. 81 – 9 = ☐

j. 81 ÷ 9 = ☐

Time taken ☐ seconds.

This shape is a ☐

Quick Change

a.£1 – 56p= ☐

b.£1 – 38p= ☐

c.£1 – 29p= ☐ d.£1 – 2p = ☐

e.£1 – 42p= ☐ f. £5 – £2.50 = ☐

g. £5 –£2.60 = ☐

h. £5 –£3.20 = ☐

i. £5 –£3.19 = ☐

j.£10 –£6.72 = ☐

This shape is a ☐

Time taken ☐ seconds.

DECIMAL CAKES

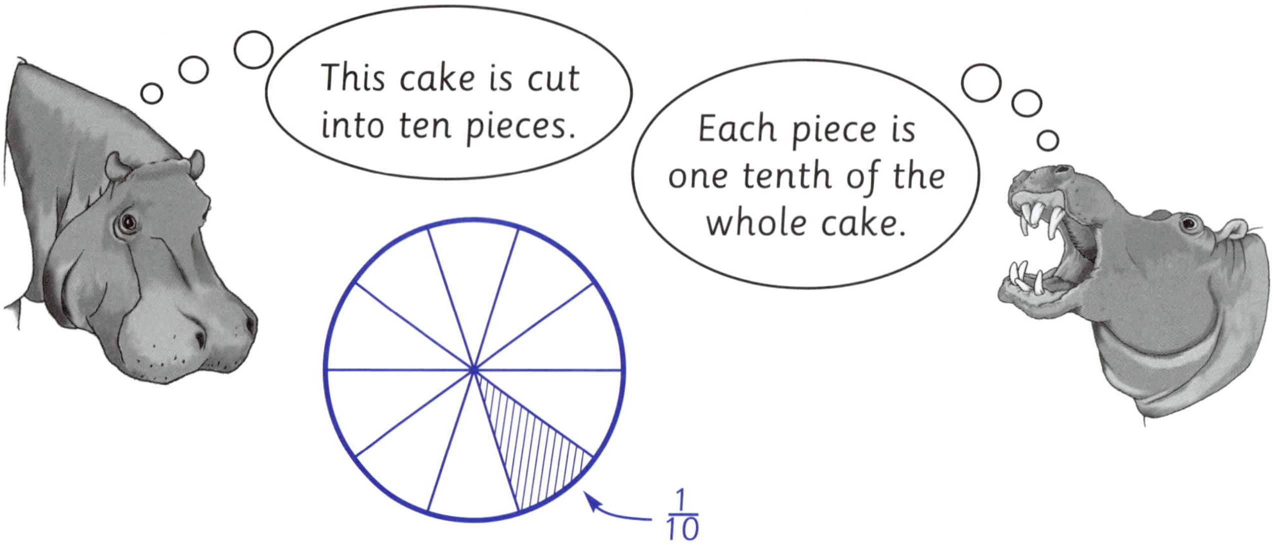

One tenth can be written like this: $\frac{1}{10}$ (a fraction)
or like this: 0·1 (a decimal)

Two tenths can be written like this: $\frac{2}{10}$ (a fraction)
or like this: 0·2 (a decimal)

Write the correct fractions and decimals for each of these cakes:

A

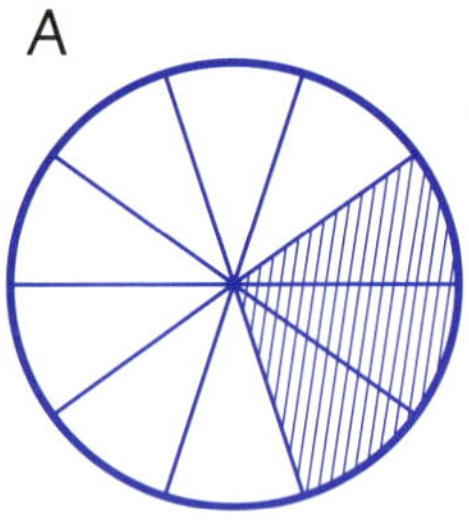

Fraction shaded ☐
Fraction unshaded ☐
Decimal shaded ☐
Decimal unshaded ☐

B

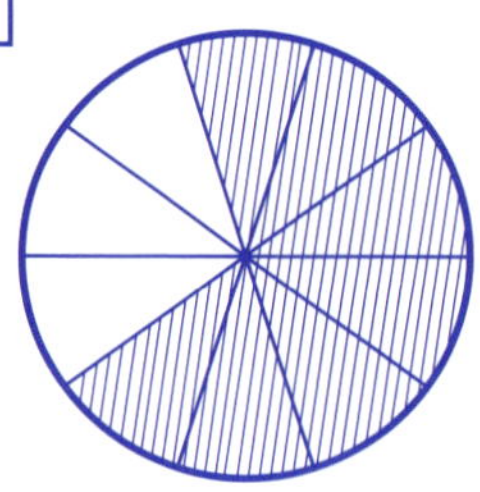

Fraction shaded ☐
Fraction unshaded ☐
Decimal shaded ☐
Decimal unshaded ☐

Look at this example:

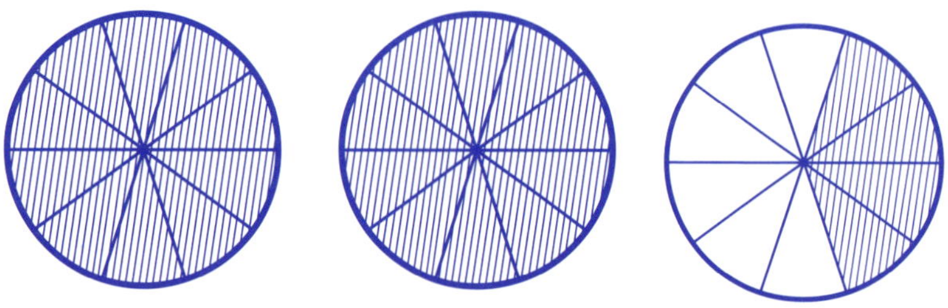

Amount shaded = 2 whole ones and four tenths.
= $2\frac{4}{10}$ (this is called a mixed number.)
= 2·4 (this is called a number with one decimal place.)

FINDING THE DIFFERENCE

What's the difference between 5008 and 3991?

Do you mean how much bigger is 5008 than 3991?

Look at this number line:

3991 is 9 less than 4000.

5008 is 8 more than 5000.

To find the difference:

1. Add 9 to get to 4000.
2. Add 1000 to get to 5000.
3. Add 8 to get to 5008.

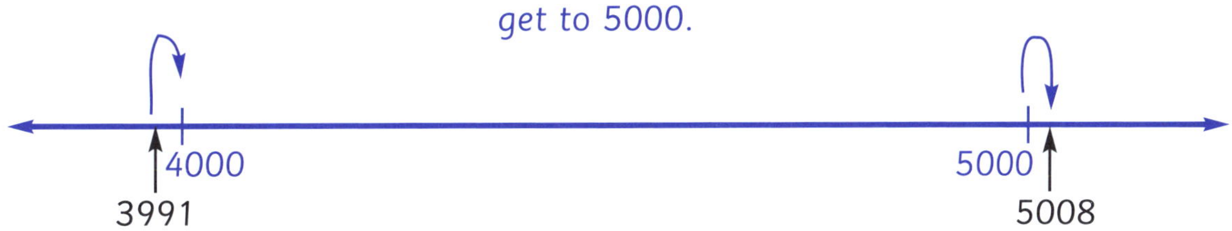

To get from 3991 to 5008 we added: 9 then 1000 then 8

⟶ that's 1017 altogether.

You may like to draw number lines to help you with these questions:

a. How much bigger is 4007 than 2998?

b. How much smaller is 1992 than 3015?

c. What's the difference between 8007 and 6994?

d. What's the difference between 3997 and 7002?

e. How much bigger is 9009 than 6996?

f. How much smaller is 2900 than 6100?

g. What's the difference between 5950 and 8020?

h. How much bigger is 5023 than 2999?

i. How much less than £5.10 is £3.98?

PERIMETER

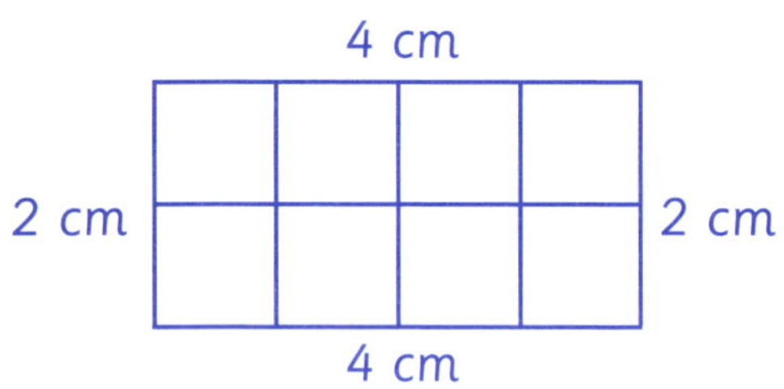

If Arnold walks all around this shape he will travel 12cm because:

4cm + 2cm + 4cm + 2cm = 12cm.

We say that the **perimeter** of the shape is twelve centimetres.

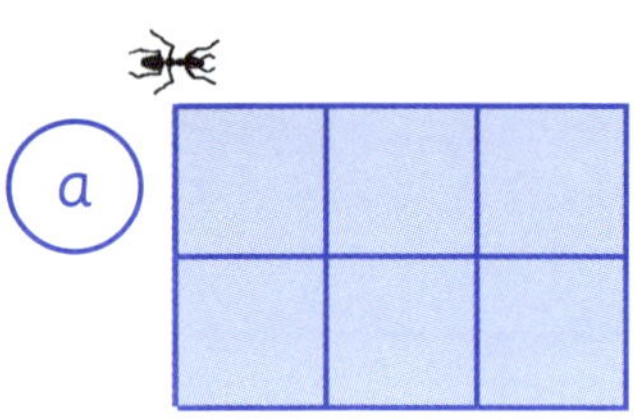

Perimeter = ☐ cm.

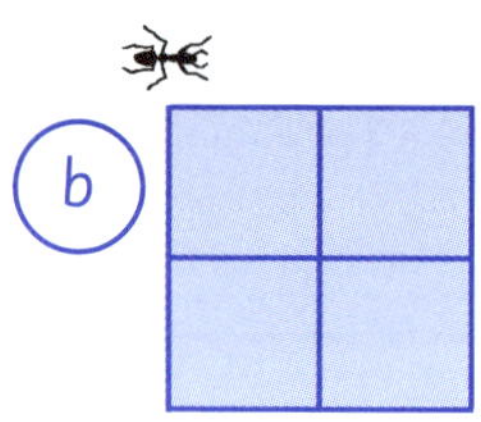

Perimeter = ☐ cm.

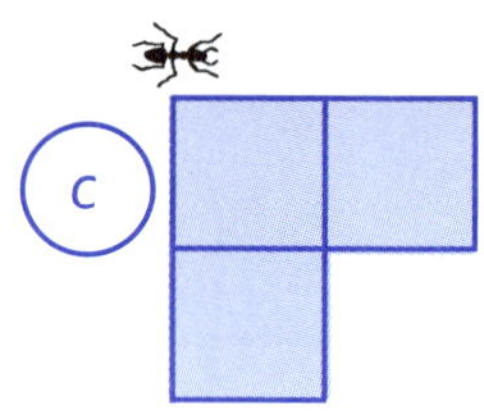

Perimeter = ☐ cm.

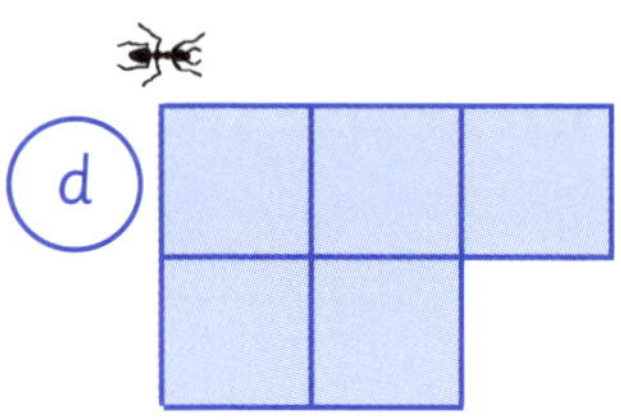

Perimeter = ☐ cm.

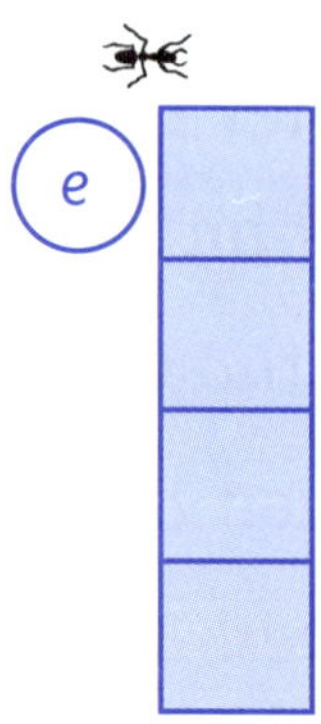

Perimeter = ☐ cm.

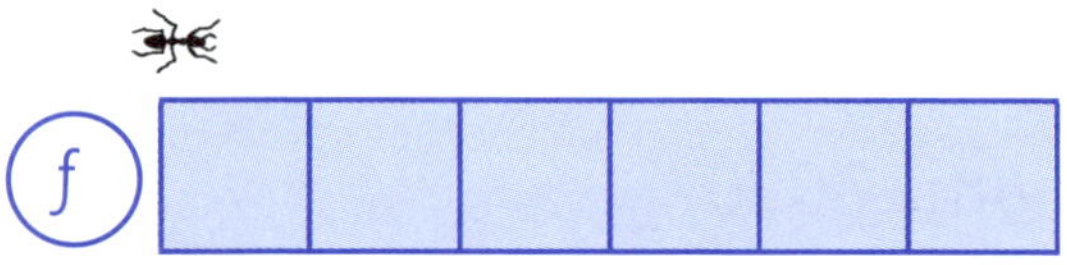

Perimeter = ☐ cm.

Perimeter = ☐ cm.

FRACTIONS

Match the shaded part of the shape to the fraction and the words. The first one is done for you. Copy the words to learn the spellings.

one quarter		$\frac{1}{9}$
two thirds		$\frac{1}{4}$
one ninth		$\frac{5}{8}$
three sevenths		$\frac{2}{3}$
five eighths		$\frac{2}{5}$
two fifths		$\frac{3}{7}$

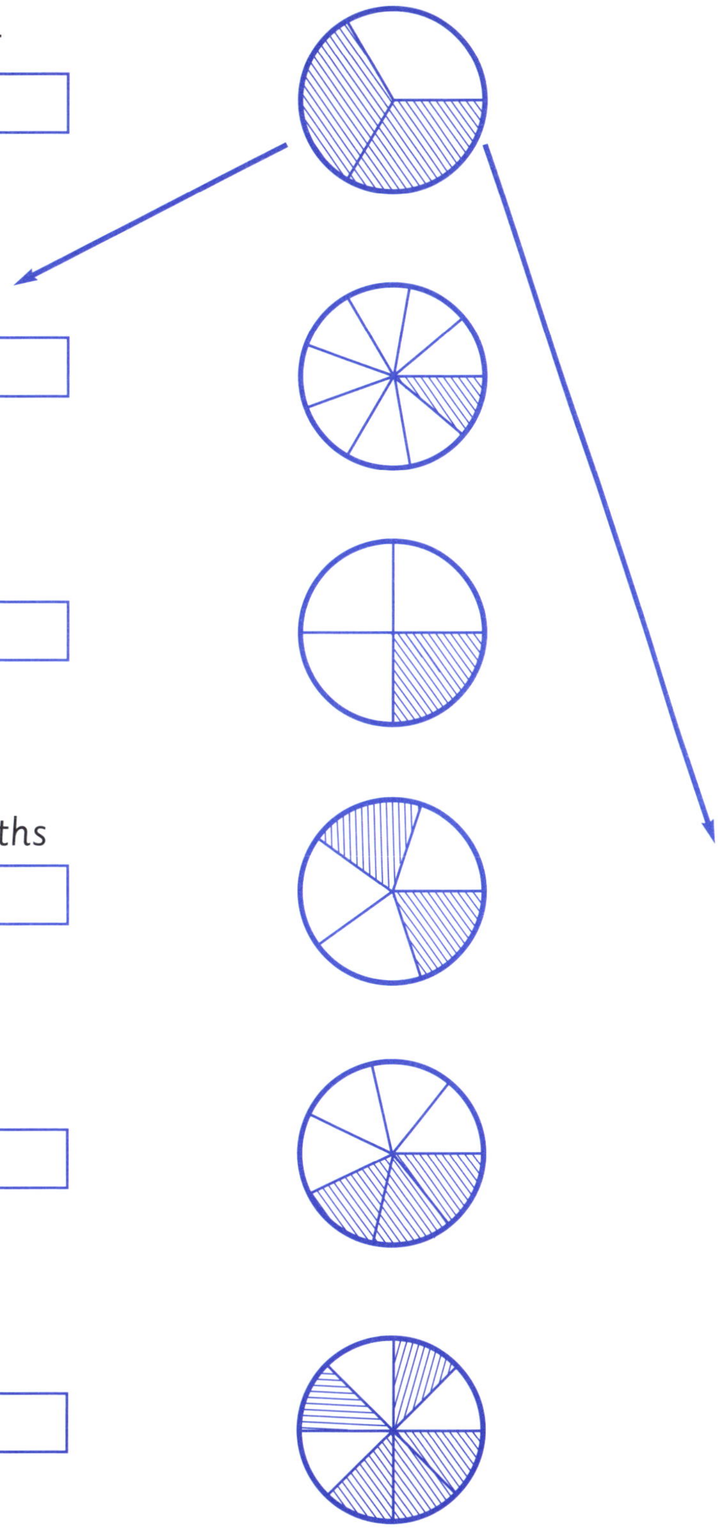

TEACHERS & PARENTS

During their literacy work in Year 5, your children will build on the work they have done in Years 1 to 4. They will experience the daily Literacy Hour in which they will examine a range of texts, produce purposeful pieces of writing and learn about aspects of spelling and grammar. The lessons will include work on:

- ✓ A range of spelling strategies, including words ending in vowels other than 'e', the prefixes trans, auto, bi, tele & circum, and using dictionaries and spell checks;
- ✓ Using and spelling possessive pronouns;
- ✓ Homophones (words with same pronunciation but different spellings);
- ✓ Effective use of punctuation in longer sentences;
- ✓ Understanding the layout of written dialogue;
- ✓ Use of adverbs in writing dialogue;
- ✓ Idiomatic phrases;
- ✓ Word roots;
- ✓ Investigating word order;
- ✓ Synonyms;
- ✓ Direct and reported speech;
- ✓ Comparison of poetic styles;
- ✓ Metaphors;
- ✓ Note taking, including the use of simple abbreviations;
- ✓ Writing and evaluating play scripts;
- ✓ Use of pronouns.

Introductory work for many of the above points will be found in the literacy pages of this book.

TECHNICAL VOCABULARY

This page is concerned with some of the words you will hear during your literacy lessons in Year Five. You should know what they all mean.

Follow the clues to complete the word snakes. The words you will need are at the bottom of the page.

1. A word indicating the position of something. E.g. in, on, between.
2. Conversation between two or more people.
3. A word showing how a verb is carried out. E.g. She ran quickly.
4. Words such as she or he that can be used in place of a noun.
5. Word with the same pronunciation but different spelling and meaning. E.g. road, rode.
6. A word that means the same, or nearly the same, as another word.
7. Words that sound as they mean. E.g. splash.
8. Commas, etc.
9. A passage of writing.
10. Describing an item as though it is something else.

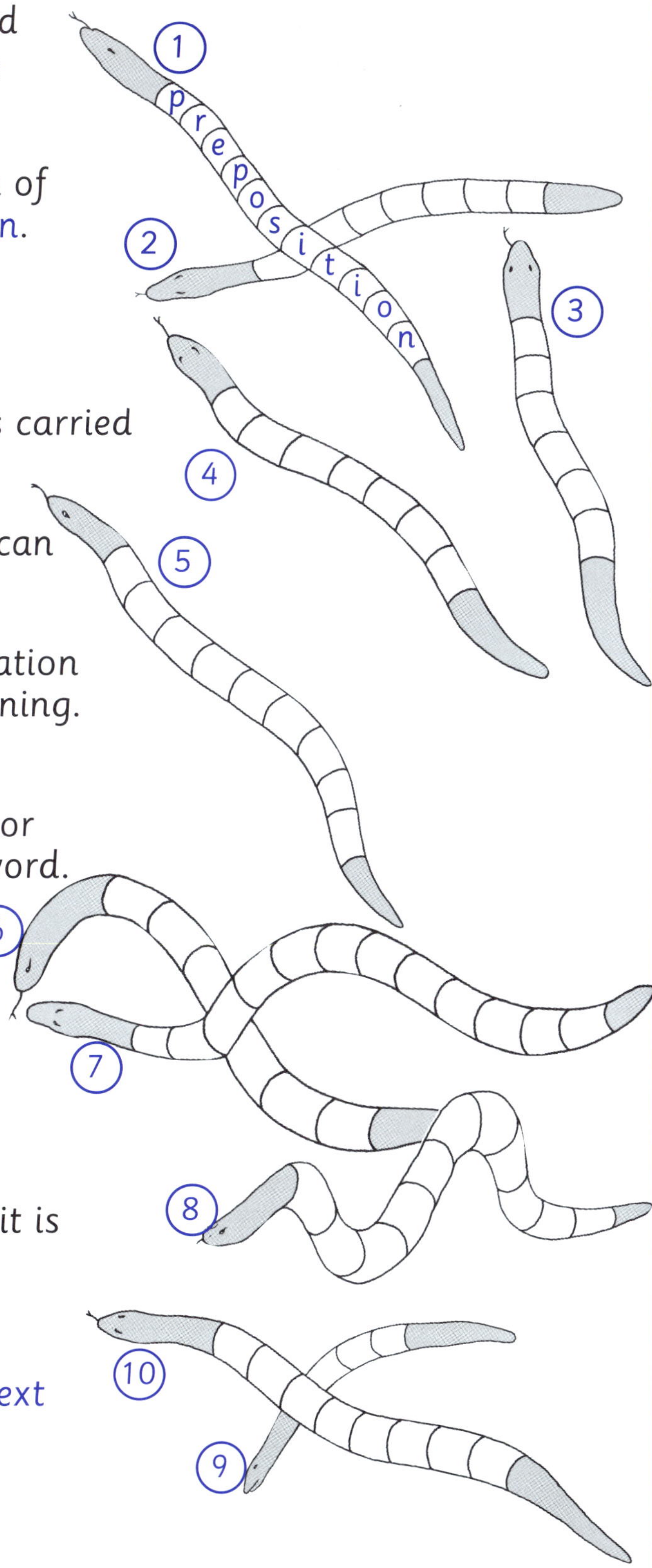

preposition adverb text

punctuation metaphor

dialogue homophone synonym

pronoun onomatopoeia

WRITING DIALOGUE

It is important to set out written dialogue correctly. Remember these simple rules.

- ✍ Use speech marks before and after the words spoken.
- ✍ Use a new line and a new sentence each time a different character speaks.
- ✍ Put a comma, a question mark or exclamation mark between the direct speech and the words describing who was speaking and how they spoke.

Here is an example of correctly written dialogue.

> "Look at that elephant!" he exclaimed.
> "Where?" she asked.
> "Over there by the large old tree," he replied, pointing in the direction she should look.

Use the lines provided to rewrite the following text correctly.

I'm frightened whispered Kelly anxiously. Kim replied softly don't worry I wont leave you here in the dark, I'll walk home with you. Thank you said Kelly with obvious relief in her voice I'm glad I won't have to walk home alone. The two friends walked along the dark quiet street until they reached Kelly's home. Thank you for walking with me she said as she went into the house. See you tomorrow replied Kim before disappearing into the dark November evening.

HOMOPHONES

Homophones have the same pronunciation, but they are differently spelled and have different meanings.
Choose the correct word to put in each of the sentences below.

pair or pear

1. I bought a new _ _ _ _ of trousers yesterday.

2. I would like to eat a sweet juicy _ _ _ _ .

rode , rowed or road

3. He ran along the _ _ _ _ .

4. I _ _ _ _ _ the boat across the river.

5. My brother _ _ _ _ a horse yesterday.

pane or pain

6. I had a _ _ _ _ in my side.

7. The _ _ _ _ of glass was broken.

steal or steel

8. _ _ _ _ _ is a type of metal.

9. It is wrong to _ _ _ _ _ .

alter or altar

10. I will _ _ _ _ _ my shirt to make it smaller.

11. The _ _ _ _ _ is at the front of the church.

sell or cell

12. I am going to _ _ _ _ my old toys.

13. The prisoner was locked in a _ _ _ _ .

C AND G

The letter c can sound soft (like an s) or hard (like k).
A soft c is often followed by an i.

Sort the following words into those with a hard c and those with a soft c. Some words might belong in both categories.

citrus	scale	mice	Mexico
crust	circle	cinema	accident
city	circus	niece	cake

Hard c

Soft c

The letter g can also make a soft sound (like j). A soft g is often followed by an e.

gun	giant	goat	goal	gift
great	hedge	gem	gerbil	ginger
giblets	dragon	grin	gear	

Hard g

Soft g

Page 5 MULTIPLYING BY 10 OR 100
a.40, b.340, c.250, d.990, e.160, f.500, g.7000, h.60000, i.7, j.58, k.19, l.100000, m.800, n.400, o.1600, p.4800, q.7900, r.4000, s.90, t.960, u.100.

Page 6 PRACTISING MULTIPLICATION TABLES
See inside the back cover for answers.

Page 7 MORE MULTIPLICATION TABLES PRACTICE
See inside the back cover for answers.

a.8, b.8, c.4, d.9, e.5, f.4, g.3, h.8, i.4, j.9
a.7, b.6, c.8, d.7, e.3, f.9, g.9, h.9, i.8, h.9
a.6, b.8, c.2, d.9, e.4, f.7, g.3, h.5, i.10, j.1

Page 8 POSITIVE AND NEGATIVE NUMBERS

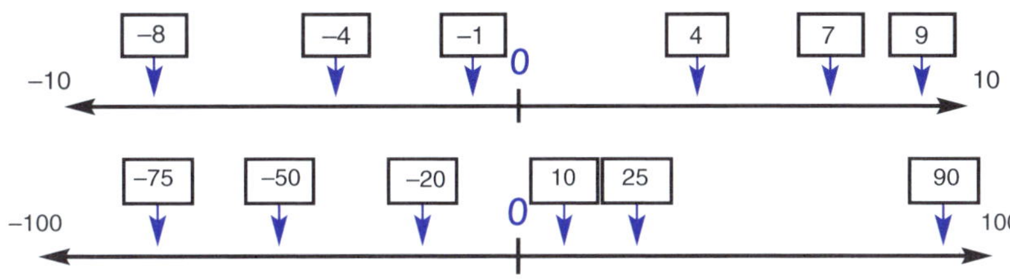

To get from –2 to 5 = 7

Page 9 MONTHS AND YEARS
January 31, February 28/29, March 31, April 30, May 31, June 30, July 31, August 31, September 30, October 31, November 30, December 31.
30 days - April, June, September and November.
31 days - January, March, May, July, August, October, December.
Days in 1 year - 365, in leap year - 366.
Years in decade - 10, in century - 100.
Years in millennium 1000.

Page 10 FAST WORK
Quick Subtractions a.19, b.26, c.11, d.7, e.9, f.7, g.32, h.22, i.12, j.2, k.50, l.49 Shape is a rectangle.
Quick Additions a.15, b.12, c.16, d.12, e.15, f.25, g.35, h.75, i.13, j.33, k.93, l.103 Shape is a square.
Quick Doubles a.12, b.18, c.10. d.24, e.28, f.40, g.30, h.100, i.50 Shape is a triangle.

Page 11 MORE FAST WORK
Quick Halves a.10, b.15, c.20, d.25, e.30, f.35, g.40, h.45, i.50, j.13, k.14, l.18 Shape is a pentagon.
Quick Mixture a.10, b.13, c.32, d.35, e.63, f.48, g.8, h.5, i.72, j.9 Shape is a hexagon.
Quick Change a.44p, b.62p, c.71p, d.98p, e.58p, f.£2.50, g.£2.40, h.£1.80, i.£1.81. j.£3.28
Shape is a heptagon.

Page 12 DECIMAL CAKES

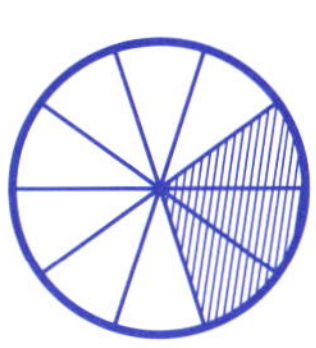

Fraction shaded = $\frac{3}{10}$
Fraction unshaded = $\frac{7}{10}$
Decimal shaded = 0·3
Decimal unshaded =0·7

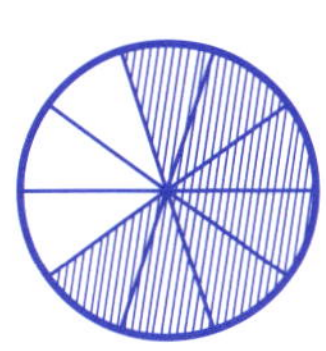

Fraction shaded = $\frac{7}{10}$
Fraction unshaded = $\frac{3}{10}$
Decimal shaded = 0·7
Decimal unshaded =0·3

Page 13 Finding the Difference a.1009, b.1023, c.1013, d.3005, e.2013, f.3200, g.2070, h.2024, i.£1.12

Page 14 Perimeter a.10cm, b.8cm, c.8cm, d.10cm, e.10cm, f.14cm, g.12cm

Page 15 Fractions

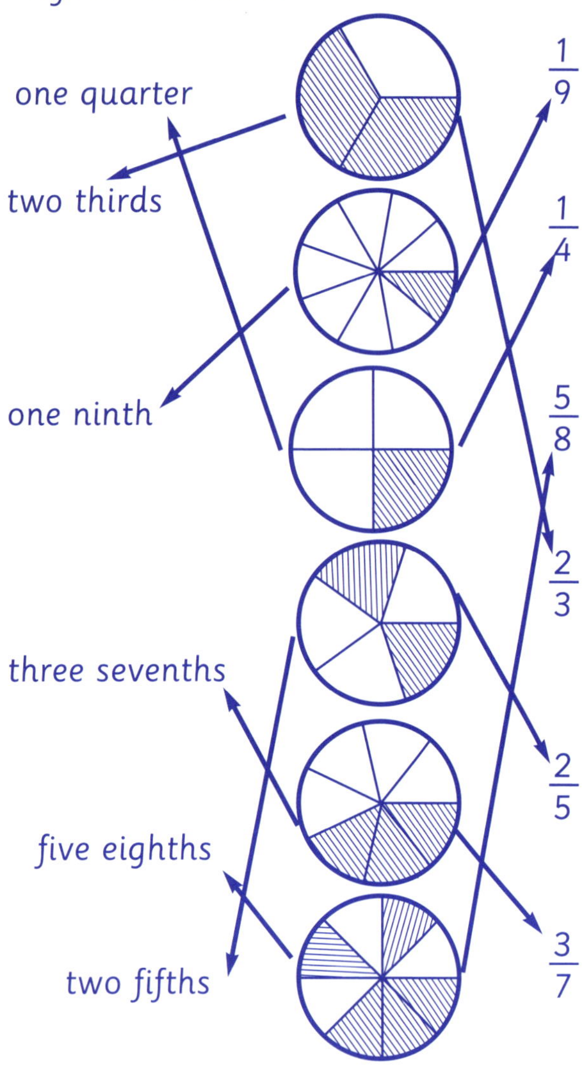

Page 17 Technical Vocabulary

1. preposition, 2. dialogue, 3. adverb, 4. synonym, 5. homophone, 6. pronoun, 7.onomatopoeia, 8. punctuation, 9. text, 10. metaphor.

Page 18 Writing Dialogue

"I'm frightened," whispered Kelly anxiously. Kim replied softly, "Don't worry, I won't leave you here in the dark. I'll walk home with you."

"Thank you," said Kelly with obvious relief in her voice, "I'm glad I won't have to walk home alone."

The two friends walked along the dark quiet street until they reached Kelly's home. "Thank you for walking with me," she said as she went into the house.

"See you tomorrow," replied Kim before disappearing into the dark November evening.

Page 19 Homophones

1.pair, 2.pear, 3.road, 4.rowed, 5.rode, 6.pain, 7.pane, 8.steel, 9.steal, 10.alter, 11.altar, 12.sell, 13.cell.

Page 20 C'S and G'S

Hard C scale, Mexico, crust, circle, accident, circus, cake.

Soft C citrus, mice, circle, cinema, accident, city, circus, niece.

Hard G gun, goal, goat, gift, great, dragon, grin, gear.

Soft G giant, hedge, gem, gerbil, ginger, giblets.

Page 21 Idiomatic Phrases

Bury your head in the sand.

Pigs might fly.

Bury the hatchet.

Don't count your chickens before they're hatched.

Can't see the wood for the trees.

It's water under the bridge.

The penny drops.

Page 22	Word Roots	mill - millstream, miller, millstones, windmill. form - information, formula, inform, formal. plant - planter, plantation, plantain, implant. act - reaction, react, active, action. 1.react, 2.plantation, 3.millstones, 4.inform.
Page 23	Words Ending in 'O'	1.kangaroo, 2.piano, 3.tomato, 4.volcano, 5.potato, 6.igloo, 7. tattoo, 8.echo. piano - pianos, volcano - volcanoes potato - potatoes, igloo - igloos tattoo - tattoos, echo - echoes
Page 24	Unstressed Vowels	separate, dictionary, factory, jewellery, Wednesday, generally, library, February, poisonous, boundary, miserable, definitely, voluntary, business, literature. Message reads - Always check with care, the vowels you need to use to spell long or tricky words.
Page 25	Words Ending in A, I or U	tarantula, gnu, paella, Hindu, ski, haiku, banana, ecru, corgi, camera, umbrella, spaghetti. Alphabetically, banana, camera, corgi, ecru, gnu, haiku, Hindu, paella, ski, spaghetti, tarantula, umbrella. questions - corgi, umbrella, haiku, camera
Page 26	Commas	1.Finn was reading his favourite book, the one about the lion, when his mother told him to come for tea. 2.Shelley's brothers, Owen and Simon, were waiting for the bus. 3. He bought a new pair of trainers, white ones with a green trim, for running in the marathon. 4 I like dogs, particularly spaniels, as they are such good company. 5.There was a wonderful feast, enough for at least fifty people, laid out on the table.
Page 27	Abbreviations	and, pound, avenue, mister, United Kingdom, kilometre, street, personal computer, number, kilogram, saint, road, Royal Air Force, for example, television, compact disc, digital versatile disc, police constable, doctor, euro.

Page 28 **Using Abbreviations** 1.I play games on my P.C. 2. Mr Brown lives at No. 19 Firs Ave. 3.I bought 2 kg of bananas, and then carried them 1 km. 4. We enjoy watching T.V. and listening to C.D.s 5. I live in the U.K., but my friend lives in the U.S.A. 6. Mister Smith lives at one hundred and one Low Street. 7. My dad is a police constable and my aunt is a doctor. 8. One thousand metres is equal to one kilometre. 9. In the street where I live there are seventy-eight houses, two public houses and Saint Margaret's church. 10. I love to read books and watch television.

Page 32 **Water** The gas we breathe is OXYGEN.

Page 33 **Your Heart and Pulse** Pulse at rest should be between 70 and 100 beats per minute. Pulse after exercise should be quicker.

Ask an adult to check your pulse rate for you.

Your heart and pulse rate increases during exercise.

Page 34 **Parts of a Flower** The male part of the flower is called the stamen. It consists of the anther and the filament. The female part of the flower is called the carpel. It consists of the stigma, the style and the ovary.

Page 36 **Musical Groups** choir, unison, harmony, quartet, quintet, brass band, wind band, orchestra, hundred, brass, string, percussion, woodwind, conductor, musicians, instrumental.

Page 37 **Muslim Beliefs and Worship** Muslims believe that God sent earlier prophets including Abraham and Jesus, but that **Muhammad** was the last one and was given the complete and final message from God.

Page 39 **Alphabetical Quiz 2** a. invented the telephone. b.Famous pop group. c. sailed to America in 1492. d. circumnavigated the world. e. Queen who reigned from 1558 to 1603. f. Famous nurse. g. Precious metal. h. Tudor king. i. An ancient civilisation. j. one of the wives of Henry VIII. k. wrote 'The Water Babies'. l. Political group, founded in 1900. m. Queen of Scots. n. Charles Dickens. o. Sporting event. p. Greek mathematician. q. married to Prince Albert. r. Marconi. s. Flagship of Christopher Columbus. t. Place of worship for Ancient Greeks. u. An ancient Greek God. v. reigned from 1837 to 1901. w. Columbus thought India. x. This form of imaging was discovered in 1895. y. Russian Cosmonaut. z. Supreme God of the Ancient Greeks.

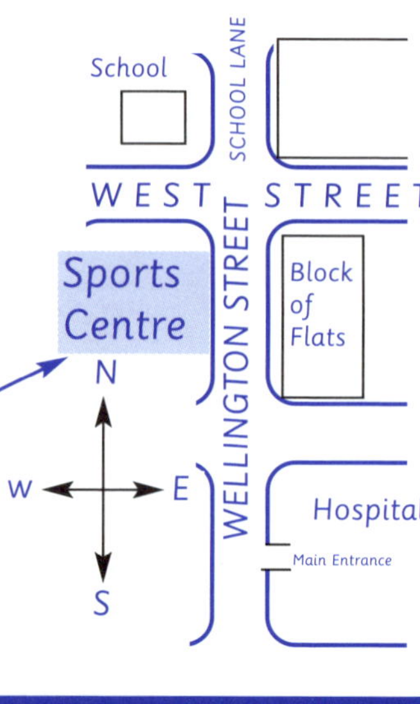

Page 40 **Street Plan** 1.Charity Shop, 2.Clothes Shop, 3.Fruit & Veg, 4.East, 5.North, 6a.West, 6b.3 shops, 7.left, 8. Sports Centre as marked on map.

IDIOMATIC PHRASES

An idiomatic phrase has words that do not give the actual meaning of the phrase. The English language has many of these phrases and we usually know what is meant when they are used.
For example when someone has very unrealistic ideas we might say they are in cloud cuckoo land.

Match each of these phrases to the definitions provided below.

The penny drops.

It's water under the bridge.

Bury your head in the sand.

Can't see the wood for the trees.

Bury the hatchet.

Pigs might fly.

Don't count your chickens before they're hatched.

Ignore a problem by pretending it does not exist.

____

This would be exceedingly unlikely to happen.

____

Resolving differences of opinion.

____

Do not rely on things that are not yet certain.

____

Unable to see the whole situation because of all the small problems within it.

____

Things that are in the past.

____

Reaching a sudden understanding.

____

WORD ROOTS

Many words use the same 'root'. Use the words in the box to complete the 'word trees'. The first one has been started for you.

planter	millstream	reaction	information	formula	react
miller	active	plantation	millstones	plantain	
windmill	action	inform	formal	implant	

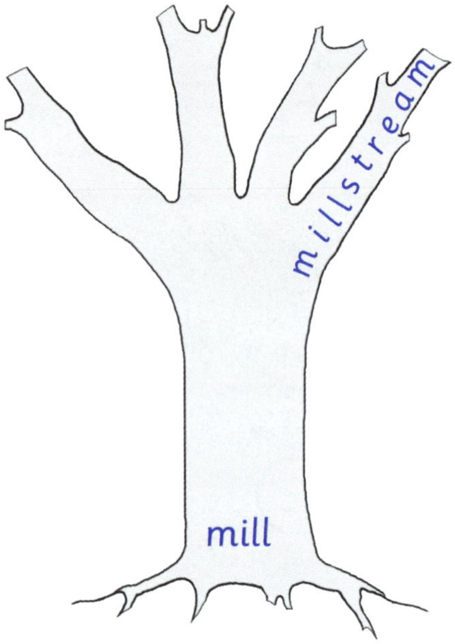

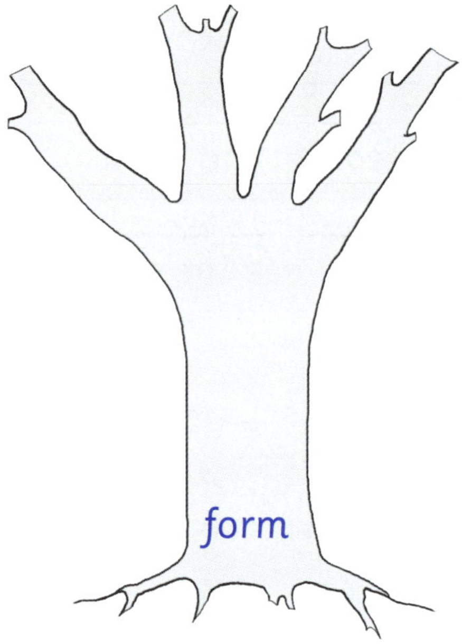

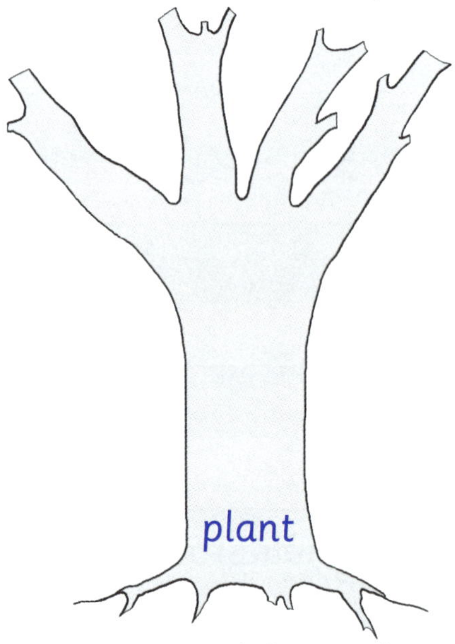

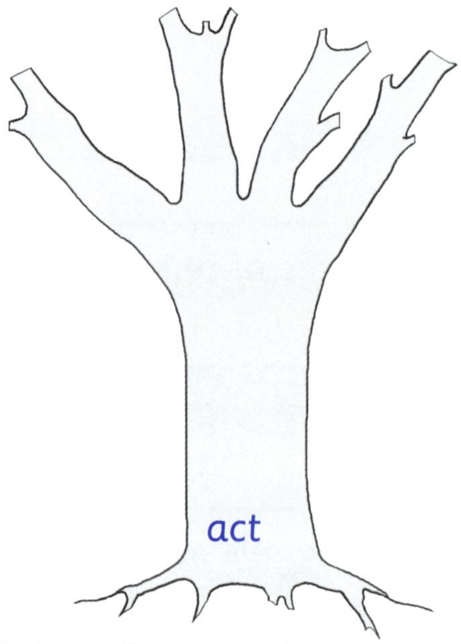

Match a word from above to each of the following definitions.

You may need a dictionary to help you.

1. To act in response to something.
2. An area, like a farm, full of crops, eg. bananas or tea.
3. Two large flat stones used to grind grain.
4. To give information.

WORDS ENDING IN O

Use each of the letters on the dice only once, to discover 8 words ending in o. There is a clue to help you find each word.
The number that follows the clue tells you how many letters are in the word.

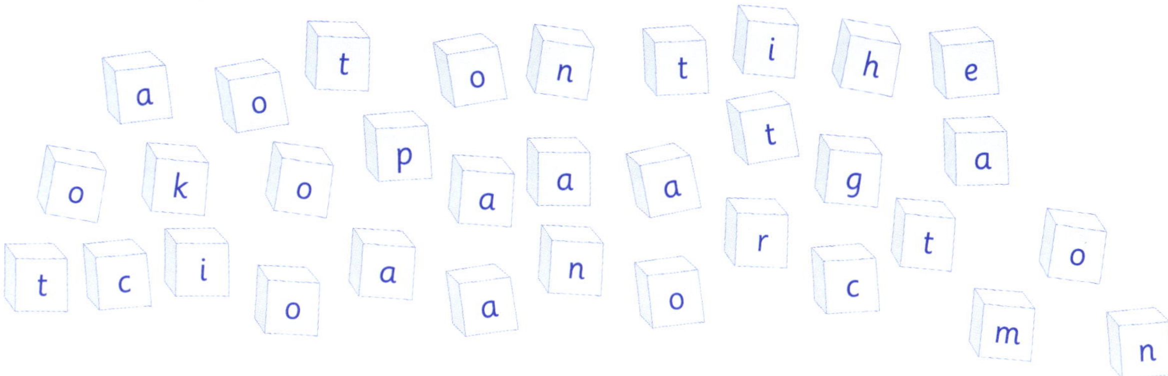

1. Australian jumping marsupial. (8) _ _ _ _ _ _ _ _
2. Musical instrument with black and white keys. (5) _ _ _ _ _
3. Red, juicy salad ingredient. (6) _ _ _ _ _ _
4. Erupting mountain. (7) _ _ _ _ _ _ _
5. Root vegetable, may be mashed. (6) _ _ _ _ _ _
6. Ice house. (5) _ _ _ _ _
7. A picture or pattern on one's skin. (6) _ _ _ _ _ _
8. The reflection of a sound. (4) _ _ _ _

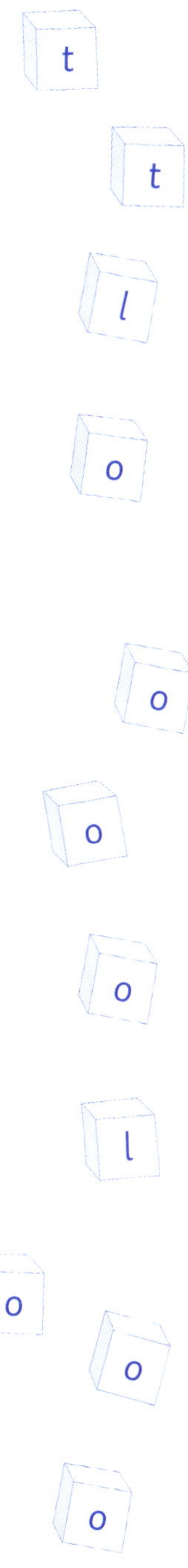

Now write each of the words again below, and put its plural beside it.
Two have been done for you.

kangaroo	→	kangaroos	tomato	→	tomatoes
______	→	______	______	→	______
______	→	______	______	→	______
______	→	______	______	→	______

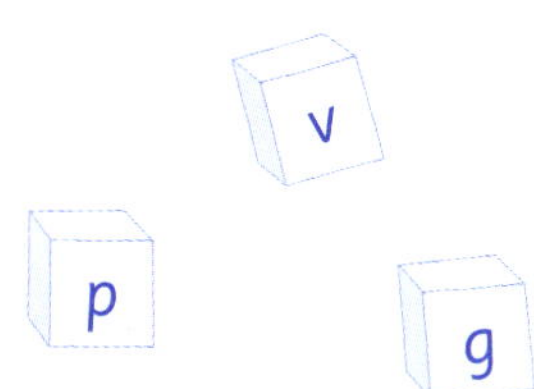

UNSTRESSED VOWELS

The vowels have been left out of the words below.
Put in the missing vowels, and then check your answers by finding the words in the word search. Shade each word in the word search as you find it.

s _ p _ r _ t _	d _ ct _ _ n _ ry	f _ ct _ ry
j _ w _ ll _ ry	W _ dn _ sd _ y	g _ n _ r _ lly
l _ br _ ry	F _ br _ _ ry	p _ _ s _ n _ _ s
b _ _ nd _ ry	m _ s _ r _ bl _	d _ f _ n _ t _ ly
v _ l _ nt _ ry	b _ s _ n _ ss	l _ t _ r _ t _ r _

s	e	p	a	r	a	t	e	a	l	j	q	x	b	o	u	n	d	a	r	y	w	a	z	y
s	z	x	d	c	h	q	z	e	x	e	q	c	k	z	z	d	q	q	x	x	z	x	q	f
x	q	z	e	z	x	w	z	x	i	w	q	z	x	q	l	i	t	e	r	a	t	u	r	e
x	z	x	f	z	q	x	z	x	z	e	t	x	h	z	q	c	c	z	z	a	z	x	q	b
b	u	s	i	n	e	s	s	r	q	l	e	x	f	a	c	t	o	r	y	z	t	x	z	r
h	z	e	n	x	z	z	v	o	x	l	z	x	w	q	e	i	z	x	z	l	x	q	x	u
s	x	z	i	q	y	x	o	z	u	e	q	q	z	n	x	o	x	e	e	x	q	l	q	a
d	q	t	t	o	x	q	z	u	q	r	z	x	s	z	e	n	z	t	z	o	z	i	s	r
p	e	w	e	d	n	e	s	d	a	y	l	z	l	q	x	a	q	l	x	o	n	b	g	y
z	o	q	l	x	z	x	r	q	z	x	t	g	e	n	e	r	a	l	l	y	x	r	z	r
i	z	x	y	c	v	o	l	u	n	t	a	r	y	z	x	y	q	z	x	q	z	a	q	k
z	x	y	q	z	z	x	q	z	w	z	x	o	m	i	s	e	r	a	b	l	e	r	x	q
q	x	p	o	i	s	o	n	o	u	s	q	x	r	z	d	x	q	x	z	z	x	y	q	s

When you have shaded all 15 words in the word search you must colour every x, q and z.
The remaining letters, reading each line from left to right, will spell out a message. Write it below.

_ _ _ _ _ _   _ _ _ _ _   _ _ _ _   _ _ _ _,   _ _ _   _ _ _ _ _ _

_ _ _   _ _ _ _   _ _   _ _ _   _ _   _ _ _ _ _   _ _ _ _

_ _   _ _ _ _ _ _   _ _ _ _ _.

WORDS ENDING IN A, I OR U

Read along the word string to find 12 words, all of which end in A I or U. Write them in the spaces provided.

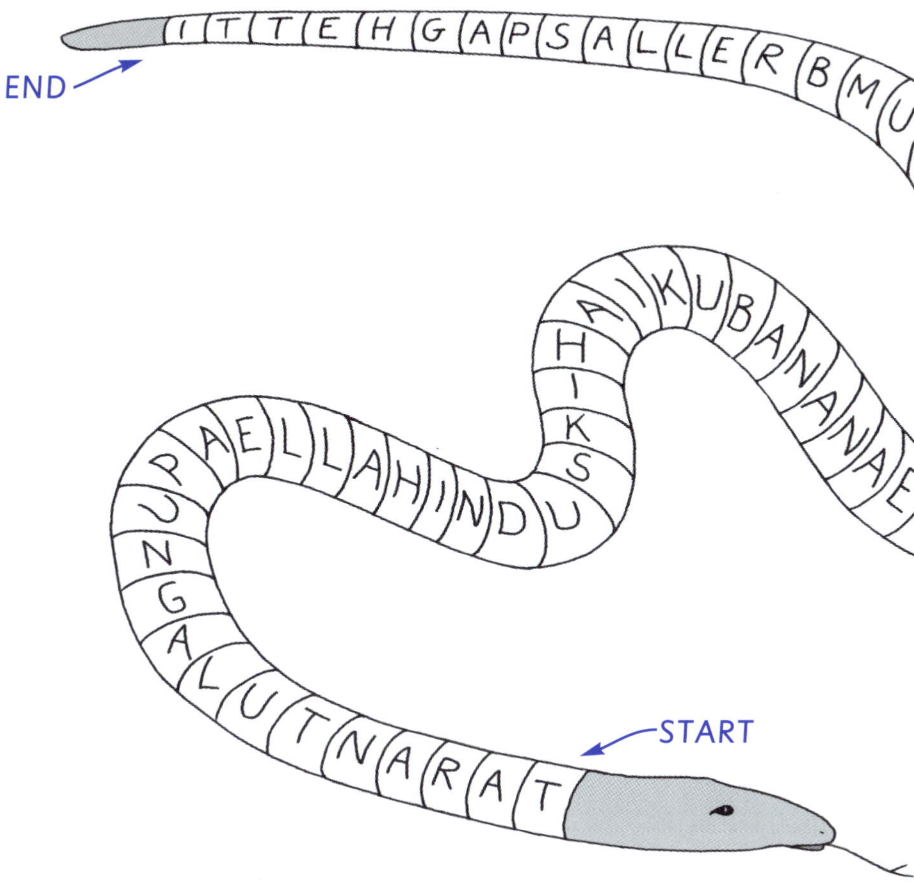

__________ __________ __________ __________

__________ __________ __________ __________

__________ __________ __________ __________

Now sort them into alphabetical order.

1. __________ 2. __________ 3. __________ 4. __________

5. __________ 6. __________ 7. __________ 8. __________

9. __________ 10. __________ 11. __________ 12. __________

Match the correct word to each of the following definitions.

A breed of dog. _ _ _ _ _

A hand-held cover for protection from the rain. _ _ _ _ _ _ _ _

A type of poem that has 17 syllables. _ _ _ _ _

A device used to take photographs. _ _ _ _ _ _

COMMAS

Sometimes a separate clause inside a sentence is marked with commas.
For example –

> Zac loved to go to school, rarely missing a day, as he enjoyed learning new things.

Rewrite each of the following sentences, in your best handwriting, inserting the missing commas, capital letters and full stops.

1. finn was reading his favourite book the one about the lion when his mum told him to come for tea

2. shelley's brothers owen and simon were waiting for the bus

3. he bought a new pair of trainers white ones with a green trim for running in the marathon

4. i like dogs particularly spaniels as they are such good company

5. there was a wonderful feast enough for at least fifty people laid out on the table

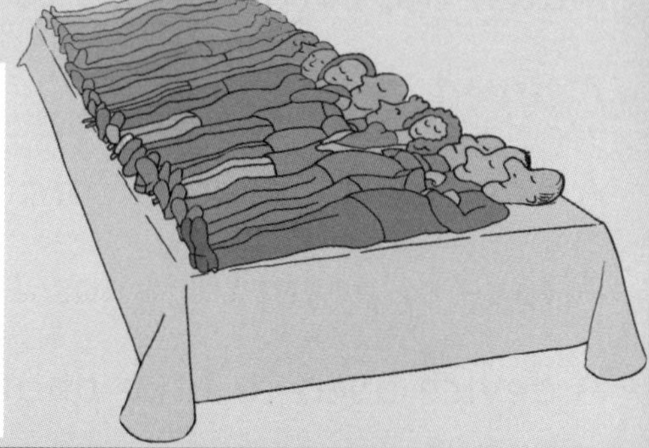

ABBREVIATIONS

Abbreviations are shortened ways of writing words or phrases. Often sets of initial letters are used to save time writing words. When you are jotting notes it can be very useful to use some abbreviations. Many abbreviations should have full stops after some or all of the letters but, in the modern style of writing them, we often do not use the full stops.

From the box, choose the correct words to match the commonly used letters and symbols below.

number	television	kilogram	police constable
pound	mister	kilometre	personal computer
digital versatile disc	and	doctor	United Kingdom
compact disc	avenue	street	saint
Royal Air Force	euro	road	for example

&		St.	
£		Rd	
Ave		R.A.F.	
Mr		E.g.	
U.K.		TV	
km		CD	
St.		DVD	
PC		PC	
No.		Dr.	
kg		€	

USING ABBREVIATIONS

When writing notes, using abbreviations can save time and space.

Rewrite the following five sentences using abbreviations where possible.

1. I play games on my personal computer.

2. Mister Brown lives at number nineteen Firs Avenue.

3. I bought two kilograms of bananas, and carried them one kilometre.

4. We enjoy watching television and listening to compact discs.

5. I live in the United Kingdom, but my friend lives in the United States of America.

Now rewrite the following five sentences using full words to replace the symbols, figures and letters used to abbreviate them.

6. Mr. Smith lives at 101 Low St.

7. My dad is a P.C. & my aunt is a Dr.

8. 1000m = 1Km.

9. In the St. where I live there are 78 houses, 2 pubs & St. Margaret's Church.

10. I ❤ to read books & watch T.V.

The National curriculum shows that every child in Year 5 needs to be taught Science and the 'foundation subjects', Art, Design Technology, Geography, History, Information Technology, Music and Physical Education, together with Religious Education.

✓ SCIENCE

Pupils are likely to learn about keeping healthy, particularly in relation to the heart and blood circulation. They will learn about life cycles of plants and animals, naming parts of a flower and considering reproduction. In learning about materials they will study the difference between gases, solids and liquids, and they will make observations of the 'changes of state' from solid to liquid to gas. The children will learn some facts about the Earth, the Moon and the Sun. They will carry out investigations, experiments and observations in relation to sound and how it travels.

✓ DT

The Design Technology work may be linked to the science and music curriculum as the children may focus on creating simple musical instruments. The Year 5 programme for DT also includes work on food, specifically bread, biscuits and other baked products. In studying mechanisms the children may investigate producing a moving toy that includes a cam.

✓ IT

Provided the school has the appropriate computers and software, the children will learn how to manipulate 'objects' on the screen, creating then changing shapes and copying and moving these shapes, perhaps to make a collage for printing out. The pupils will make use of simple databases to sort information and to print out graphs, and they will begin to learn how to use spreadsheets for processing information. They may also have the opportunity to use IT for controlling electrical devices such as motors and lights.

MAKING BREAD 1

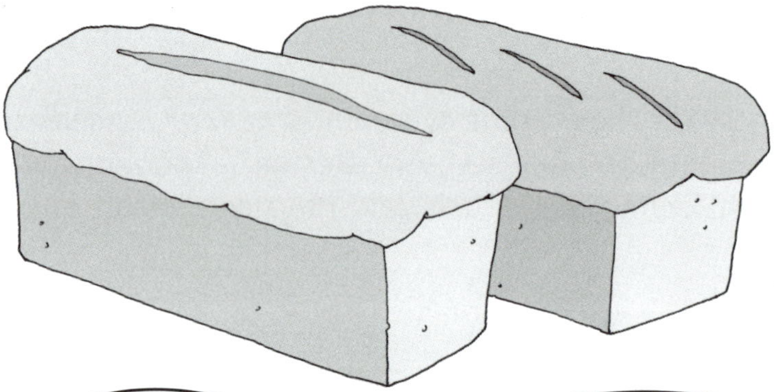

Ingredients

750g Wholemeal flour
4 level teaspoons of salt
1 packet of easy bake yeast (7g packet)
1 tablespoon of olive oil
450ml warm water

Method

1. Put the flour, the salt and the yeast into a bowl.
2. Mix them together.
3. Pour in the tablespoon of olive oil.
4. Pour in the warm water.
5. Use your hands to mix the ingredients together. They should make a big ball of soft **dough**.
6. Sprinkle some flour onto a flat surface.

MAKING BREAD 2

7. Lift the dough onto the flat surface and keep turning it over and pressing into it with your fists. This is called **kneading**. You should knead the dough for three minutes.

8. Spread some olive oil over the inside surface of a loaf tin.

9. Put the dough into the loaf tin, then leave it in a **warm** place. Ask an adult to turn on the oven to Gas Mark 7 or to 220°C.

10. You should check the dough after half an hour. If it has grown to double its size it's ready to bake. If it hasn't grown, you should leave it in the warmth for longer.

11. When the dough is ready, ask an adult to put it in the oven. It will be very hot so you must have the help of an adult.

12. After 35 minutes ask an adult to put on some oven gloves and to take the loaf out of the oven.

13. Leave it to cool, then take it out of the loaf tin and eat it.

WATER

The air around us is a gas. It's made of a mixture of other gases, including oxygen, carbon dioxide and water vapour. Find out which one of these we need to breathe in every time we take a breath. [ ]

YOUR HEART AND PULSE

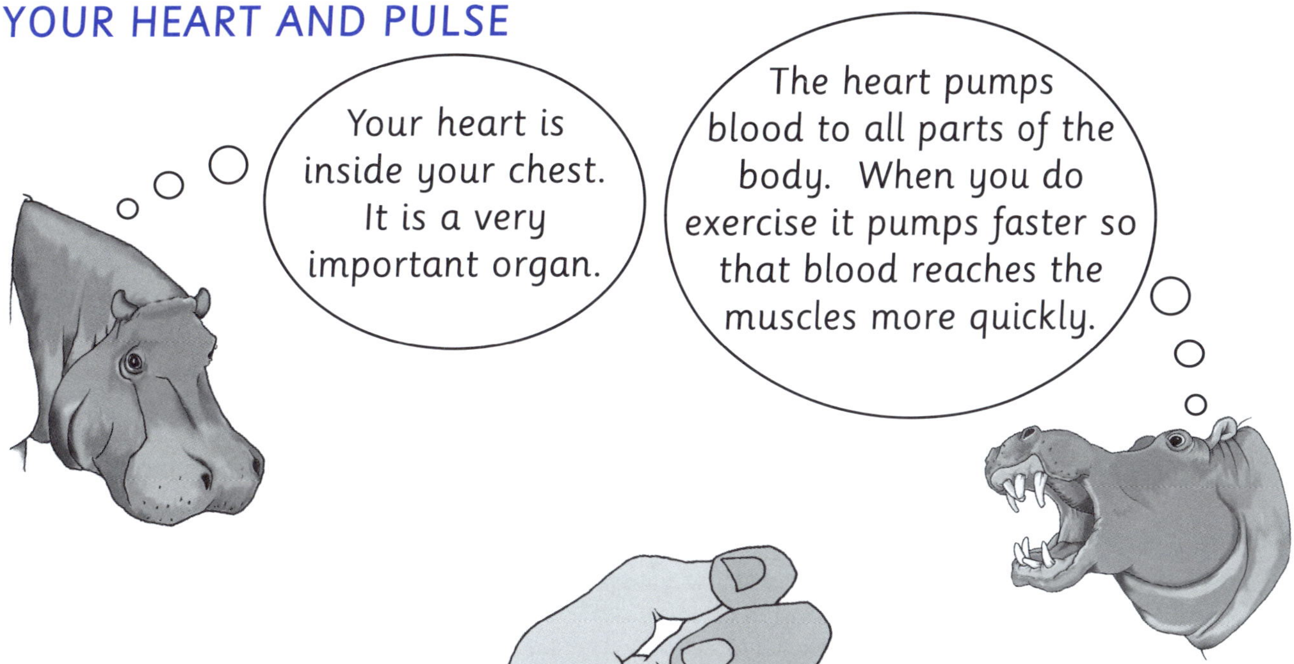

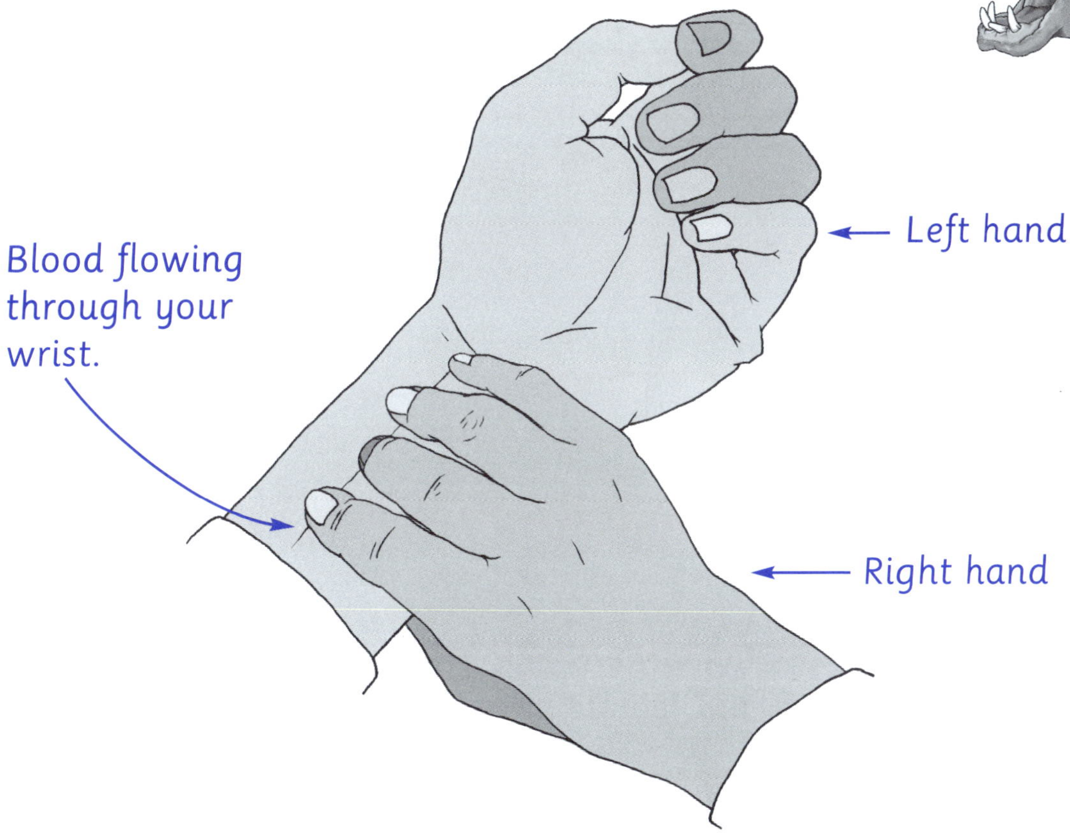

If you feel very carefully with the fingers of one hand you can find the **pulse** of your blood passing through the wrist of your other hand.
Don't press too hard, just feel gently.
When you have found the pulse, try counting the beats for exactly one minute, by timing yourself using a watch with a second hand.

How many **beats per minute** did you feel? ☐

Now do some exercise for about one minute.
You could run on the spot or skip with a rope.
Find your pulse again. Try counting your beats per minute now.

What score do you find? ☐

How has this changed? ____________________

PARTS OF A FLOWER

Female parts

The **stigma**, **style** and **ovary** are female parts. Together they are known as the **carpel**.

Male parts

The **anther** and **filament** are male parts. Together they are known as the **stamen**.

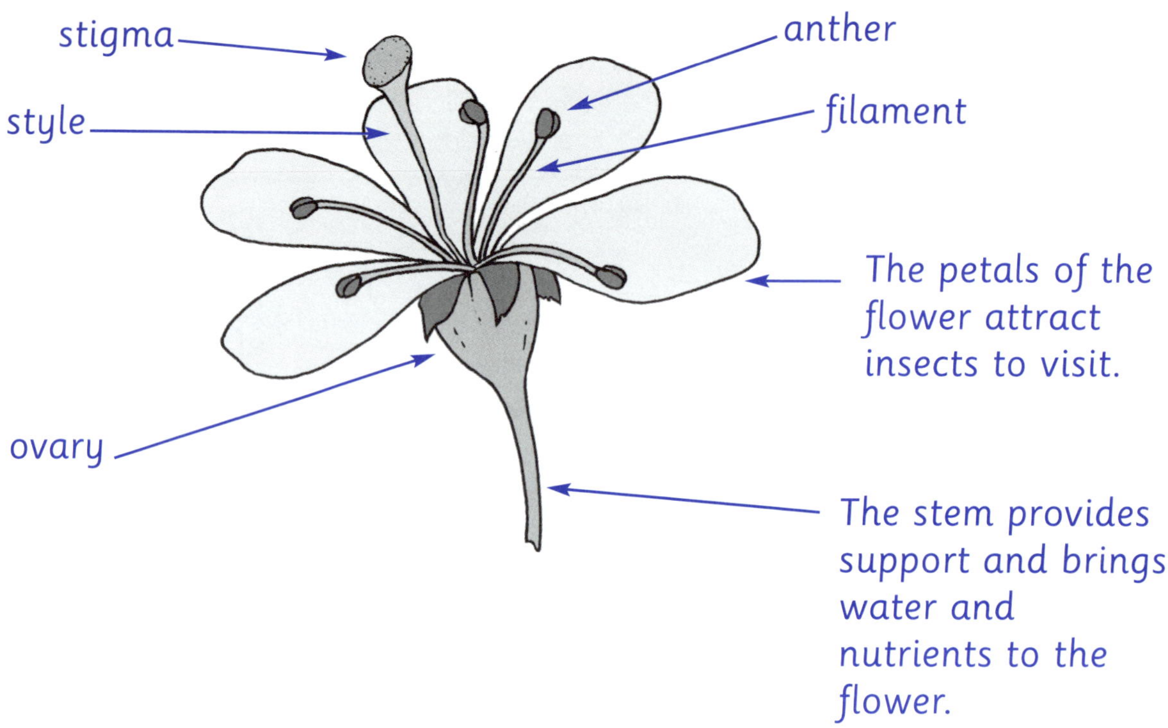

For most plants the reproductive organs can be found in the flowers. The flowers have male parts and female parts. Pollen is produced by the male part, at the anther.

When an insect such as a bee visits the flower, the pollen rubs on to the bee's body. The bee may then visit another flower where the pollen rubs off the bee and on to the stigma, which is one of the female parts. In this way the flower becomes pollinated and can then begin to form seeds. These seeds can grow into new plants.

The information on the diagram will help you to fill in these missing words:

The male part of the flower is called the ☐. It consists of the ☐ and the ☐.

The female part of the flower is called the ☐.

It consists of the ☐, the ☐ and the ☐.

TEACHERS & PARENTS

✓ MUSIC

During Year 5, pupils will be building on the musical understanding and skills they have developed in Years 1 to 4. They will be focusing on their performance skills using their voices and a range of instruments. To help pupils to gain most benefit from this work, this book includes work on understanding some of the musical vocabulary they will encounter.

✓ RE

In Year 5, pupils are likely to study the lives and worship of Christians and Muslims. The work in this book is based on the latter.

✓ HISTORY

In Years 5 and 6, aspects of some or all of the following topics may be studied: Tudor exploration, Victorian Britain, Life in Britain since 1948, The Indus Valley Civilisation and Ancient Greece. The history pages in this book consist of a challenging quiz which may take several days to complete. Solving the quiz will provide worthwhile opportunities for research in books or on the computer.

✓ GEOGRAPHY

Pupils will make increasing use of atlases, maps and globes. They will be encouraged to take note of news and current affairs, using maps to identify places featured. Maps such as street plans will also be used when comparing the local area to a contrasting area within the United Kingdom. Pupils may take part in an extended study in relation to water and how it is used in this country and abroad. They will consider the local area, possibly focusing on the traffic in their town centre.

✓ ART

In Years 5 and 6, children will be asked to create a still-life painting based on objects they have chosen - through this they will make use of their sketchbook of work and will learn various techniques for working with paint. To experience three-dimensional art they may be asked to make a container using clay or to make headgear or a costume for a character in a story. They will work with textiles to make pictures that tell stories and will learn about the use of art for story-telling - the Bayeux Tapestry, for example. The pupils will extend their art work in creating pictures that show movement and in studying landscape artists as a stimulus for their own work.

✓ PHYSICAL EDUCATION

Pupils are likely to participate in a wide variety of PE activities including:

- 'Invasion Games' in which they have to enter another team's territory and score goals;
- 'Striking and Fielding Games', such as cricket or rounders - they may not take part in full games but will be practising the necessary skills of throwing, catching and hitting a ball;
- 'Net or Wall Games', such as short tennis, badminton and possibly volleyball;
- Gymnastics, showing increasing control and agility;
- Athletics, including throwing, running and jumping;
- Dance, learning different styles and working with partners or in groups.

MUSICAL GROUPS

Musicians very often perform in groups. The writing below is about different sorts of musical groups.
Choose words from the box at the bottom of the page to fill the gaps in the text.

A group of singers is known as a ______. When all the singers sing the tune, or melody, this is known as singing in ______, and when they sing different notes at the same time it is called singing in ______.

There are many different sizes and types of instrumental groups. When four singers or instrumentalists perform together it is called a ______, and when there are five in the group it is a ______. A ______ ______ is a group of players playing brass instruments with just the addition of percussion. When the group includes brass and woodwind with percussion it is a ______ ______.

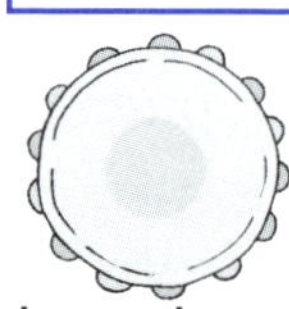

Perhaps the best-known type of instrumental group is the ______. These can range from a small one with only about 25 players, to a large modern orchestra with over a ______ musicians.

Whatever size an orchestra is it always has four main sections. These are the ______ section the ______ section the ______ section and the ______ section. The players in an orchestra are usually arranged in a semicircle enabling all the players to have a clear view of the ______.

Most ______ enjoy playing in a group. If you enjoy singing, or are able to play an instrument, perhaps you too would enjoy being part of a choir or an ______ group.

orchestra, brass band, musicians, choir
harmony, quartet, hundred, string
conductor, woodwind, percussion, unison
wind band, brass, quintet, instrumental

MUSLIM BELIEFS AND WORSHIP

Read the following facts about what Muslims believe and how they worship. When you have read the text carefully you will be ready to complete the puzzle. Each of the words in black type has its letters in the boxes below. Shade out the letters for each word and you will be left with the letters needed to fill the space in the final sentence.

Muslims are followers of the faith known as **Islam**.

They believe there is only one God, called **Allah**.

The **prophet** Muhammad is important to Muslims, as they believe he was the final messenger sent by Allah.

It is important to understand that Muslims do not actually **worship** Muhammad.

Angels gave God's messages to Muhammad.

Muslims believe that each person has **two** angels watching over them.

Muhammad learned God's messages by heart, and these form the holy writings known as the **Qur'an**.

The Qur'an is written in **Arabic**, and is always read in that language.

Muslims **pray** five times each day.

The prayer times are **dawn**, midday, late afternoon, evening and finally at the end of the evening.

We have started the puzzle for you, by shading the letters for the first word, ISLAM.

I	L	P	S	L	W	T	C	M	A	E	A
A	O	T	H	O	I	S	E	M	A	R	D
A	N	A	A	B	U	I	M	D	R	Y	R
L	N	H	S	W	L	O	R	P	H	M	A
A	P	W	Q	H	R	A	G	U	P	N	A

If you have shaded the letters in all the words written in bold you should be left with the letters that will complete the sentence below.

Muslims believe that God sent earlier prophets including Abraham and Jesus, but that _ _ _ _ _ _ _ _ _ was the last one and was given the complete and final message from God.

ALPHABETICAL HISTORY QUIZ 1

On this page you will find 26 clues to correctly match to the answers on the following page. Write the key words from each clue carefully on the line provided beside the answer.

An ancient Greek God (a planet is named after him).

Precious metal that many 15th and 16th century explorers hoped to find.

Invented by Marconi in the Victorian era.

Famous pop group in which John Lennon played.

Christian name of one of the wives of Henry VIII.

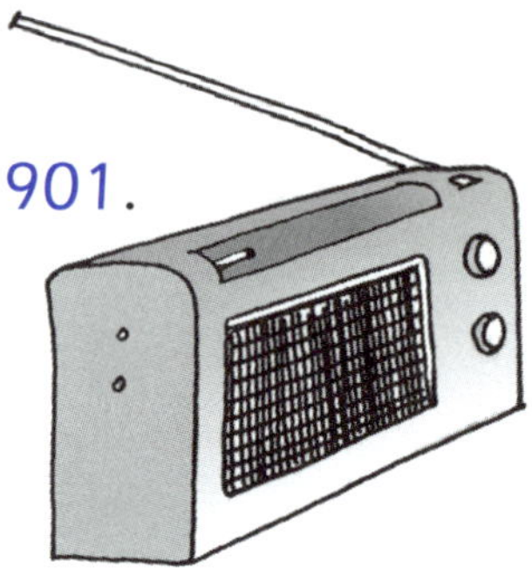

Sporting event originating in Ancient Greece.

The first name of the queen who reigned from 1837 to 1901.

Famous nurse from Victorian period.

Flagship of Christopher Columbus.

Russian cosmonaut, made the first manned space flight.

An enemy of Queen Elizabeth I, known as _______ Queen of Scots.

Victorian inventor who invented the telephone.

Supreme God of the Ancient Greeks.

Novel written by the Victorian author Charles Dickens.

This form of imaging was discovered in 1895 (used in hospitals).

Political group, founded in 1900.

Columbus thought that these islands were off the coast of India.

This Elizabethan circumnavigated the world.

Explorer who sailed to America in 1492.

An ancient civilisation lived in part of the area we now call Pakistan.

Queen who reigned from 1558 to 1603.

Place of worship for Ancient Greeks.

Tudor king who married six times.

Famous Greek philosopher and mathematician.

She was married to Prince Albert.

Victorian author who wrote 'The Water Babies'.

ALPHABETICAL HISTORY QUIZ 2

Write the correct clue from the previous page, beside each answer.

Alexander Graham Bell ______________________

Beatles ______________________

Christopher Columbus ______________________

Drake (Francis) ______________________

Elizabeth 1st ______________________

Florence Nightingale ______________________

Gold ______________________

Henry VIII ______________________

Indus Valley ______________________

Jane ______________________

Kingsley (Charles) ______________________

Labour Party ______________________

Mary ______________________

Nicholas Nickleby ______________________

Olympic Games ______________________

Pythagoras ______________________

Queen Victoria ______________________

Radio ______________________

Santa Maria ______________________

Temple ______________________

Uranus ______________________

Victoria ______________________

West Indies ______________________

X-Ray ______________________

Yuri Gagarin ______________________

Zeus ______________________

STREET PLAN

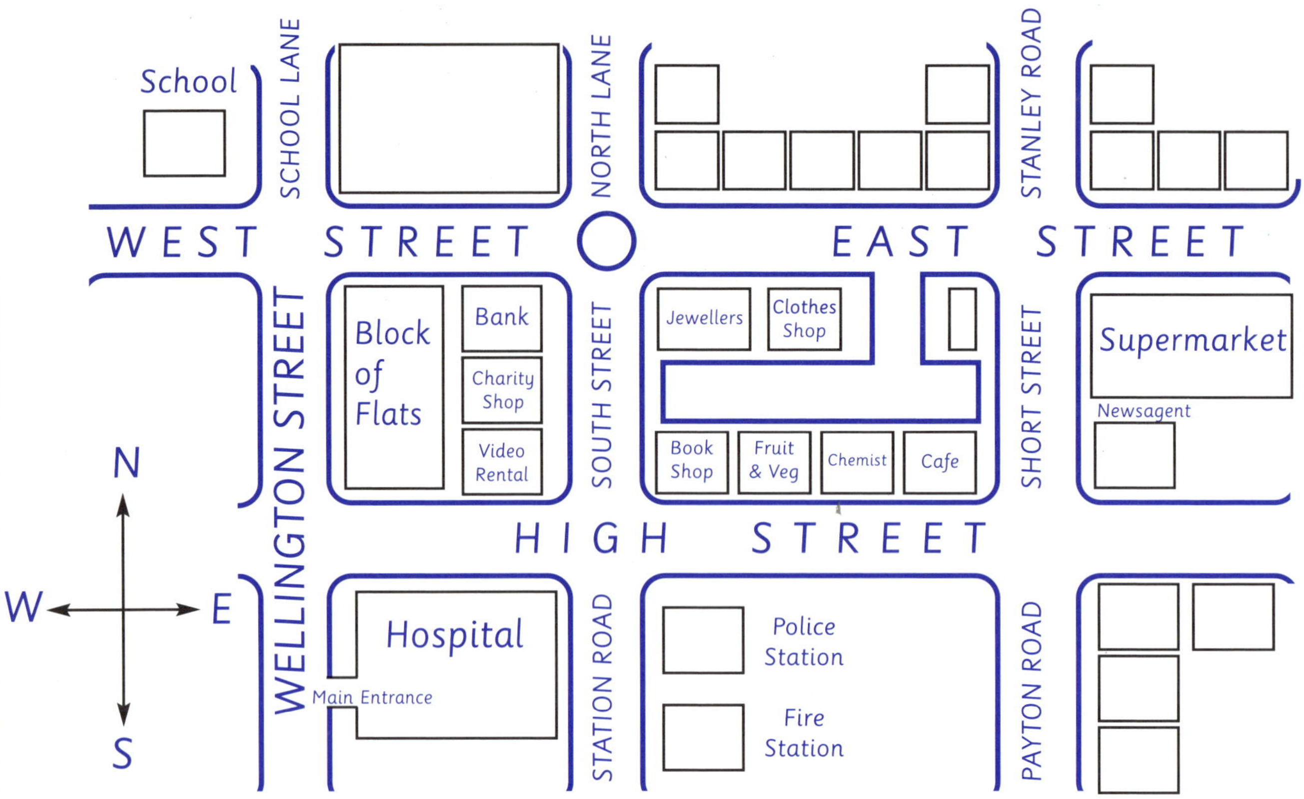

Answer these questions about the map:

1. Which shop is south of the bank?
2. Which shop is east of the jewellers?
3. Which shop is west of the chemist?
4. In which compass direction should I go to get from the video rental shop to the cafe?
5. In which direction should I go to get from the fire station to the bookshop?
6. a. If I walk from the cafe to South Street, in which direction am I walking?

   b. How many shops would I pass?
7. If I am travelling westwards along High Street do I turn right or left into Station Road?
8. Mark a Sports Centre on the map. It should be to the west of Wellington Street and to the south of West Street.